Trawling for Truths

Trawling for Truths

Don Gutteridge

Wet Ink Books

First Edition

Wet Ink Books
www.WetInkBooks.com
WetInkBooks@gmail.com

Copyright © 2022 Wet Ink Books
Copyright © 2022 Don Gutteridge

All rights revert to the author. All rights for book, layout and design remain with Wet Ink Books. No part of this book may be reproduced except by a reviewer who may quote brief passages in a review. The use of any part of this publication reproduced, transmitted in any form or by any means, electronic, mechanical, photocopied, recorded or otherwise stored in a retrieval system without prior permission in writing from the publisher or a licence from The Canadian Copyright Licensing Agency (Access Copyright) is prohibited. For an Access Copyright licence, visit: www.accesscopyright.ca or call toll free: 1.800-893-5777.

Trawling for Truth
by Don Gutteridge

Cover Design – Richard M. Grove
Layout and Design – Richard M. Grove
Cover Image – Shutterstock, used by permission
Typeset in Garamond
Printed and bound in Canada
Distributed in USA by Ingram,
   – to set up an account – 1-800-937-0152

Library and Archives Canada Cataloguing in Publication

Title: Trawling for truths / Don Gutteridge.
Names: Gutteridge, Don, 1937- author.
Description: Poems.
Identifiers: Canadiana 20220275378 | ISBN 9781989786734 (softcover)
Classification: LCC PS8513.U85 T73 2022 | DDC C811/.54—dc23

Table of Contents

- The Armour of My Arms – *p. 1*
- God's Nod – *p. 2*
- Camelot – *p. 3*
- Cocooning – *p. 4*
- For Every Favour Bestowed – *p. 5*
- Plum – *p. 6*
- Grace – *p. 7*
- Puddled – *p. 8*
- After the Fever – *p. 9*
- Angling for God – *p. 10*
- Dizzied – *p. 11*
- Estranged – *p. 12*
- A Singular Evening – *p. 13*
- Tingle – *p. 14*
- Elaborately Alive – *p. 15*
- Grit – *p. 16*
- Ambush – *p. 17*
- Chill – *p. 18*
- Summertime Stroll – *p. 19*
- Banjo – *p. 20*
- Steadfast – *p. 21*
- God's Gas – *p. 22*
- Dead-Set – *p. 23*
- A Story wth Legs – *p. 24*
- So Bright and so Fair – *p. 25*
- Hallelujahs – *p. 26*
- Heretic – *p. 27*
- A Story – *p. 28*
- Still in the Bud – *p. 29*
- Mister and Missus – *p. 30*
- Incubation – *p. 31*
- Gerry's Dad – *p. 32*
- My Town – *p. 33*
- Sagas – *p. 34*
- Haloes – *p. 35*
- On Looking Again at Keats's Odes – *p. 36*
- Ogle – *p. 37*
- This Photo – *p. 38*
- Love will Out – *p. 30*

– Requiem – *p. 40*
– Firearm – *p. 41*
– Hurdy Gurdy – *p. 42*
– Trotter – *p. 43*
– Hopes – *p. 44*
– Seasonal – *p. 45*
– Kindling – *p. 46*
– Ruby – *p. 47*
– A Valentine – *p. 48*
– Bottle – *p. 49*
– Girls' Game – *p. 50*
– Serene – *p. 51*
– Hope – *p. 52*
– Camouflage – *p. 53*
– Paradisians – *p. 54*
– Rooted – *p. 55*
– Wordsworthian – *p. 56*
– Tailor-Made – *p. 57*
– Slant – *p. 58*
– An Innocent Eye – *p. 59*
– Shockwaves – *p. 60*
– Drowned Aloud – *p. 61*
– Chintzed – *p. 62*
– When Lilacs Hung Lovely – *p. 63*
– Dervish – *p. 64*
– Something in my Throat – *p. 65*
– Love's Tug – *p. 66*
– Brooder – *p. 67*
– Odes – *p. 68*
– When I am Gone – *p. 69*
– What Is – *p. 70*
– Hunter's Heart – *p. 71*
– Somewhere – *p. 72*
– On The Road Again – *p. 73*
– Box Cars – *p. 74*
– Well-Dug – *p. 75*
– Tethered – *p. 76*

Author Biographical Note – *p. 79*

The Armour of My Arms

For Anne in loving memory

O my love! I can still
feel the feel of your flesh
and the warmth of your welcoming
on those nights when only
our bodies would do, our lust
undistilled by tact
or the little healing acts
of affection that made our days
a delight, but in the aftermath
of our mutual meshing, we lay
in the lustre of the other's light,
something immaculate aglow
in our bones, and I would forgo
half a lifetime to have you
wrapped once more in the
amorous armour of my arms.

God's Nod

Each evening, when I was
young enough to know
better, I knelt beside
my bed, palms pressed
reverent, and hoping for Heaven
chanted the child's prayer:
"Now I lay me down to sleep,"
pleased to leave my soul
in another's keep, and pausing
to breathe anew, waited
for God's approving nod.

Camelot

For Nancy, wherever she be

Nancy Mara was the first
girl to dance dactyls
in my dreams, and therein
she was ever Guin to my Lance,
and I would beguile her with the gift
of the Grail and the simmer of my smile,
but once upon a day,
between Spring and Fall, I grew
a summertime itch, so gripped
in the groin, it left me livid
with a lust too grooved
to be unbegot, while I:
no longer entranced by Camelot
or the clumsy rituals of romance.

Cocooning

The girls in my country school
were all gangling and giggle,
not a curve or wiggle in view
(or they may have been cocoons
cradling a chrysalis and waiting
for wings to gel); still,
being boys and bearing the brunt
or blame, we hungered after
something we needed to name,
and feel - like a bone in the belly.

For Every Favour Bestowed

When the Missus Bray said
her prayers each night,
she promised her God a flower
for every favour He chose
to bestow, and O how her heart
soared when their garden grew
in beauteous bloom – and the Lord's
light.

Plum

When Adam and Eve walked
the Garden in the cool of the evening,
they found nothing naughty
in their nudity or titillating
in their tender gendered parts
or lewd in the looks they lavished
on the other or awkward
when it came time to talk,
for Eden was rinsed in innocence
by the God who fashioned it,
and all went well till Eve
plucked a "plum" from the
Knowing Tree, and Adam,
lit with lust, succumbed
to her plumbing.

Grace

For my father in loving memory

Word soon got out
that a local lad was a blur
on blades with the grace of a bird
in feathered flight, who could tickle
a puck with the wisp of his stick
or make it dance like a Dervish
on adrenalin, and in the Fall
of thirty-nine, in the deepest
days of the Great Depression,
the hometown hero was given
a chance to pivot for the pros,
but he chose instead to hang up
his skates and go off to weather
the Wars, and though he returned
with his knack intact, he never
"laced 'em up" again.

Puddled

In Sunday school we gambolled
with God and sang our souls
away: of Jesus and the precious
blood of the Lamb, but all
I ever saw when I shut
my heathen eyes to seize
that wondrous sight in my gaze
was a gutted bundle and puddled
blood.

After the Fever

I was introduced to Jesus
at Sunday school, five
months after the fever
struck and put me at odds
with God, and I still remember
ambling home, paper
pamphlet in my religious
fist with a picture on it
of the man, who, though
an only-begotten son,
would save me from sin and herald
Heaven – in flowing robes,
sandaled toes, a halo
of ginger locks, and eyes
too blue to be believed,
and I too sang
"Jesus loves me," as if
the Bible could deem it so.

Angling for God

In Sunday school, we sang
of Jesus calling the Apostles
to be fishers of men, and I pictured
Simon Peter, rod-
in-hand, casting a line
into the gulp of Galilee,
hooking the souls abandoned
there and hoisting them
Heavenward, and when our Savior
bade us follow, we did,
glad to be angling for God.

Dizzied

In Hendrie's henhouse,
numbed in the summer sun
and its shine, Jo-Anne dropped
her drawers and exposed the ribald
rose where her thighs inclined,
and we were so dizzied
we couldn't tell a "mine"
from a "yours" or a "hers" from a
"his'n."

Estranged
For Dylan

You bade your father rage
against the lapsing of the light,
and yet you showed little
care for the breath of your own
body, bingeing on booze
till it soaked your bones and licked
its lips on your liver, and you found
no ease in the empty ecstasies
of philandering sex or the hermitage
of the home hills – estranged
as you were from everything but the
poems that burned still
through the alcoholic haze
of your bard's brain or oozed
perhaps onto a drink-inked
page, but at the end, I like
to think you did not go gentle
into anyone's Good Night.

A Singular Evening
September 1957

She was the gamin-next-
door, my roomie's cousin,
and I her blind date
in borrowed blazer and turbid
tie, and we danced the evening
young at Mart Kenny's
Ranch, cheek to cheek
to the music of slow trombones,
and later on, in the dark
of my buddy's car, our lips
enlisted, tongues clung,
and we let our bodies bravely
misbehave, just shy
of "oh my!" and I remember
every touch and tingle
of that singular hour,
but, alas, cannot recall
the gamin's name.

Tingle

For Sandy and that golden summer

You settled beside me in the
windowed light, letting it
linger wherever it lent
a loveliness, like sunshine
gilding a lily, your hair
a halo feathering your face,
your gaze aglow with the tingle
of mine, and I thought "Madonna"
and of Michelangelo's mystic
marbling and virgins Vestal
in flowing robes, but when
you smiled my way, something
less than holy tugged
at my soul, and I wanted only
to hug you whole.

Elaborately Alive

For Tom in loving memory

You tried so hard to un-
hitch your addiction, and have
your soul soar through the pain
of one too elaborately alive –
like a wax-winged Icarus
enamoured of the sun's stun,
and when you died, some part
of me that had dreamed you
a future with the seeds of genius
in it and embossed by the majesty
of your mind – faltered, and I was left
bereft like a bard without a ballad,
striving to find the word
that rhymed with love and its loss.

Grit

My pal Butch shouts,
"Look at the dogs doing it
on the walk!" and I see the big
male mounted in a fine
frenzy that makes his eyeballs
bulge, and the wee female
accepting her lot, and my thought is,
"So that's what 'it' is all
about," and I wonder whether
the girls I knew would grit
their teeth, and indulge.

Ambush

In the dappled demesnes of Eden
Adam in his solitude
grew bored with tulips
and hibiscus that never needed
weeding and lambs that frolicked
the afternoons away,
and God in His mercy drew
Eve out of a random rib,
and all was well with the
prenuptial nudes until
Eve ambushed an apple.

Chill

When Coop and I wade
into the Lake's chill
and let it grip hip-
high, every vessel
in our body stiffens, including
the one imploding below,
and later in the change-room
we share shy erections
(before the dreaded droop),
at ease in the other's company,
and hoping the girls next
door will have found the peep-
hole we worried there,
and like very much what
they see.

Summertime Stroll

For Sandy, again

We kissed but once, a brief
brushing of lip to lip,
more pucker than passion,
but ours was a hand-holding
romance as we strolled the summer-
time streets of our town,
and I was happy just
to have a girl like you:
blissful in the grip of her glance.

Banjo

Chatham, Ontario: 1954
For Laura Haggith

O Laura! You were the first
girl I was in lust with:
the jig of your hip-wriggling
walk and the jellied jousting
in your skin-thin jeans
left me limp with longing
and rousted something unholy
in my bones, and there was nothing
angelic in the oh-so
come-and-get-it glance
that sent me hallooing at the moon
like a love-numbed bard,
strumming on the ol' banjo.

Steadfast

Gran's kitchen, Summer
or Winter, was a season of its own:
as cozy as a cocoon, cradling
a chrysalis, or a furred feline
dozing in a dream, and my Gran —
aproned and bemused, her smile
as mellow as a new-begotten
moon – was its royal resident,
and no matter how further
afield I roamed, in head
or heart, that numinous room
remained steadfast, a distant
nook I still call "home."

God's Gas

The sonic boom that levelled
the Reverend Bell's abode
shook the panes of every
windowed room in the village,
and I arrived on the heels
of the fire brigade, all
ogle and awe, to find
nothing but ash and embers
where a house once stood,
and the good reverend, ass-
backwards on the grass, blinking
the smoulder away, surprised
to be alive and happy to have
a ready-made theme
for Sunday's sermon: Don't
tinker with God, or gas.

Dead-Set

My Gran was dead-set
against the drink, calling out
the beer-bellied denizens
of Beveridge Room and boot-
legging burrow, or tut-
tutting when the butcher's brother
staggered past our house
on his way home from the Balmoral
to beat his wife, but sometimes,
at lunch, I might find
my Gran sipping a glass
of stout to nip, she said,
dyspepsia in the bud, but the smile
she failed to disguise in the froth
that limned her lip, told me
otherwise.

A Story wth Legs
Point Edward: 1936

There was only one murder
that shocked and appalled the good
burgers of my town, that happened
the year before I was born,
but the story still had legs
long after the dust had settled;
when young Lumley, with nothing
to show but the two-dollar
dole, proposed, and the Barker
lass said "yes," but numbed
by too many humdrum days
with nothing to do but brood
and bray, he borrowed his brother's
hunting gun and shot
the bride-to-be in her hand-
me-down wedding dress.

So Bright and so Fair

For Bob in loving memory

O brother! How I long
to be once again
in that wee womb of a room,
where we lay abed against
the nip of the night, no more
than a handspan or heartbeat
apart, and hear your voice
as high and lyric as a love-
struck castrati, singing
"In the Sweet By and By,"
and as the notes of your song
dwindle in the dark between us,
hope that when you gain
that mansion so bright and so fair,
you'll find it glorious there.

Hallelujahs

In Sunday School, we sang
of Jesus, meek and mild,
who suffered child and churl
to come unto Him holy,
and the Reverend Bell assured us
of His love, whether we deserved it
or not, because the Bible seldom
lied (and that, should we seek,
we would also surely find),
and as the hopeful notes
of our song fluttered to rest
in our God-bedewed room,
I felt something like a soul
singing Inside, and could have
crooned Hallelujahs
with the best of them!

Heretic
For D.T.

O Dylan! The dance
of your long-legged dactyls,
the heretic howl you un-
lunged and the hoarse roar
of your Welsh-rung welkin
stirred in me the bardic
urge and, like you,
(when there were wolves in the
hills of Wales) I wanted
to plumb the vale of the
ancestral soul and tongue it
to the world with the triphammer
zip of one who hoped
he might be owl-wise
by altar-light.

A Story

Sometime towards the muddle
of Grade Seven, I had
a Quixotic thought: that I
ought to try my luck
at writing a novel, and so
I begged Miss Nelson
for a brand-new, unscarred
scribbler with black, "lacquered"
covers and shy blue
lines to keep my jots
from jarring, and there on page one
I carved in charismatic capitals:
BILL BRECKENRIDGE: BOY
DETECTIVE, unaware
my sleuth's moniker was very
much like my own, and just
below the daunting of those
letters, I began to unspool
my plot and the cunning of its clues,
dreaming even then
of plaudits and authorial glory,
but halfway down the fourth
page, I ran out of steam –
and story.

Still in the Bud

When I was still a lad
and my bloom still in the bud,
I had no notion of becoming
a bard to bottle my thoughts -
or flotsam my feelings in iambs
and rhyme, or spin yarns
about the local yokels
I loved for their innocent
eccentricities, but something
infanticidal broke
in that bud and the poems flowed
aglow, spun lovely
in unblooded bouquet –
from the womb of my words.

Mister and Missus

Bill Bradley, ninety
years spry, had a reserved
pew at the Barber Shop
every Saturday morning,
whether he needed a trim
or not (or another twinkle
in his eye), and two blocks
away, his missus stood
on her front stoop, wondering
whether or why or not
again, and the single word
she unlunged at the world
was a vowel no consonant
could contain.

Incubation

In my one-room country
school, as soothing as a chrysalis
in a cocoon, I eye the big
west windows, where,
in the January chill, frost-
fronds weep upwards
from the sill like an alabaster
moss on a consenting tree,
and over the blackboard's
daily grind of grammar:
Neilson's Mercator map
of the world with *Crispy Crunch*
where Melbourne ought to be,
and above it, a bordered alphabet
with an angular A, leaning
on a curling little cousin,
each letter wishing it
were a word, and only the stammer
of a Grade Three practicing
his primer unsettles the silence,
and the heat of the morning hovers us,
hoards in corners or slumps on the line
like a bedsheet, unbillowed
by a breeze, and here I spent
a thousand of my allotted
days, content to let my thoughts
and proto-poems incubate
before they buzz in my brain
like honey-combing bees.

Gerry's Dad

Gerry's Dad was a tail-
gunner, blazing away
at Junkers and Messers from the
hub of his glass-bubble
and dodging bullets that buzzed
about him like blundering bees,
while mine, safe on the ground,
waited on runways to repair
the Spits and Mustangs that limped
inland, and by and by
when it came time to talk
about the War, not once
did Gerry boast of his Dad's
bravura, and I was happy
not having to lie.

My Town

My town was so tiny
you could spit from one side
to the other and still have a bit
left to lick, but it was
enough let my boyhood
teem: where every crack
in every walk might break
your Granny's back, and every
street we trod, like the blind
thumbing Braille, remembered
who and when, and we embraced
its divers denizens with all
their follies and frailties intact,
and loved them none the less,
for they were the stuff of stories
we told to keep our souls
alive and entertain
a yawning God.

Sagas

It was a gift from my mother
(who'd already said goodbye
to her God): *Illustrated
Stories from the Bible,* and they
were my *Arabian Nights*
and *Idylls of the King,* and I plumbed them
for plots and protagonists
with an Old Testament twang,
and I giggled at Eve, naughtily
nude in her fig-leaf
frock, and nodded approval
when Joshua's braying bugle
jettisoned Jericho, and agreed
with Job that God would not
be mocked, and shuddered
when Abe uncuddled his blade
an inch from the infant's chin,
and cheered when Moses severed
the sea and freed his people
and David perpetrated
a pebble on the Big Guy's
brow, and gasped when Lot's
wife petrified in public,
and blushed when Bathsheba
didn't and the Queen of Sheba
did, and pulled for the lions
in Daniel's den and Shadrack
and the lads toasting their toes,
and when my perusal was through,
I'd gathered enough don'ts
and doings to populate
a dozen sordid sagas.

Haloes

When I was still twelve
and Heaven beckoned still,
Shirley and the girls were just
chums with haloes of hair
and elongated legs lusty
enough to run a roused
rabbit to ground, but when
I turned thirteen, something
barbarous bush-wacked
my dreams and stirred the lurid
luggage below, and many
a night was worried away
thereafter with thoughts of nibbled
lips, tushes tumped
and breasts caressed.

On Looking Again at Keats's Odes

O these melodious odes!
of a nightingale dappling
the dark with his summer song:
reminding us all of poetry's
promise and man's mortality,
a-lurk in every uneaseful
breath we broach, or of
marbled figures, frozen
forever in hope and the
In-Being of the Beauty
he embraced with his whole
tubercular, Keatsean heart.

Ogle

O how we ogled the girls,
as if we knew what to do
should they ever give us the gift
of a glance or utter the wooing
words of a single-sided
dialogue (that left us
tongue-benumbed, and content,
alas, to dream in the dark
of rogue romance and urgent
virgins.)

This Photo
Point Edward: 1943

In this photo of the
long-ago days when I yearned
to be unyoung, I am
astride my first trike
in its second-hand season,
the pedals: wooden blocks
to meet the radius of my reach
and ride the rhythmic knack
of my knees, and O those
rubberized grips I seized
in my flurried fists, and in the
blurred background between
the neighbours' houses: the bone-
white church, whose steeple
pricks the sky with Anglican
ease, waiting for its Sunday
tongue to toll – calling the
faithful home.

Love will Out

For Anne in loving memory

I wake, and feel the flotsam
of your hair afloat on the pillow
that keeps us apart, and I am
glad that once again
we have somehow dreamed
our way safely through the
doubtful demesnes of the dark
and that, when I open my eyes,
the morning sun, softening
on the sill, will be reborn,
like a bloom, on your brow,
and love will out.

Requiem

I've said goodbye too many
times in the long years
allotted me by a merciful
God, and their faces haunt
my dreams and invade my days:
grandfather, who fought
in the trenches for the king and country
he soon forsook for more
cordial climes; my Gran,
who gave me a love I could never
earn; my mother, alone
and grieving for the love she lost
but never had; my father,
who lived long enough
for the drink to undo him;
Potsy, the uncle who decided
to brother me instead; Betty,
the aunt who thought I was a
writer before I knew it;
and dear, dear Anne,
who loved me for fifty-seven
summers, as if I deserved it;
and grandson Tom,
the sanctuary of my soul,
who was, alas, too beautiful
to be; and all those friends
of my youth and wasted age
who passed me by on their way
to otherwhere, and left me
here to drift among ghosts,
and familial phantoms –
and beatify.

Firearm

For my father in loving memory

"This gun," says my Dad,
"can stun a buffalo," as I take
the thirty-ought-six
into a shaking grip, tuck
the butt snug, like Natty
Bumppo stalking a stag,
sight the target, pinned
to a nearby pine, and squeeze
the trigger with a squirrel-
eyed squint – surprised
at the throb where I thought
my shoulder was and the buckling
of my knees: "Oh my,"
my father says, "You managed
to miss the tree."

Hurdy Gurdy
Point Edward:1947

On the last dog day
of August, while I was still
hoping to make it to eleven,
Conklin's Show and Carnival
landed on our Lakeview lot –
with its Ferris Wheel like a
petrified web, spun
by a tidy spider, and its carousel,
pumping organ tunes
plump enough to rouse
the pampered ponies we rode on
like Roy or Hopalong, and its
Tilt-a-Whirl tilting us
till we wilted, and O
the midway with aromas of
flame-fried patties
and onion-sizzle and whiffs
of cotton candy – where,
for a nickel we could pick a number
on the clacking wheel and see
it spin for some other
lucky winner, or buy
a box of Cracker Jack
and munch it till the prize
arrived, or have our weight
guessed, alas, to the ounce,
and where, for a dime and little
wit, we could watch the fat
lady sit or the Siamese
sisters share a twisted
hip – but no single
scent or sight or sound
could match that full-fledged
feeling of a midway day,
churning, like a hurdy gurdy
in the heart.

Trotter

Point Edward: July 1, 1947

The Dominion Day races
drew us to the old fairgrounds
like miller moths to a high-beam
or bees to a bloom, and we were
there to see the doe-eyed
Dixie Dunham grooming
her father's trotter, Atomic,
unsure which of them
we ought to ogle first,
her or the horse, but when
the 2:20 was finally off,
it was only that long-legged
bay, a-bob in his hobbles,
with a side-to-side striding
and a will to win whom we cheered
till we drowned in our echoes -
and Dixie's darling brought home
the roses.

Hopes
For Anne in loving memory

Your mother warned you
never to marry a teacher:
she had hopes for you other
than a chalk-jockey, cowering
in a classroom and brushing
dust from his second-hand
suit, and like Browning,
she believed a lad's reach
should exceed his grasp, but found
the ambit of my ambition a foot
shy of Heaven, but I
pursued you anyway
with poetry and roses, and eloped
with her hopes.

Seasonal

That last, anodyne day
at the Lake, the water becalmed
as a second Sargasso and the breeze
barely a breath, we toss
a frisbee to and fro
in lazy loops, watching it
glide to the perfect perch
of a fingertip, or flutter like a
butterfly on booze, or ride
the arable air like a rudderless
sloop, and we are dizzied
by such summering delights,
our thoughts adrift towards
the pain of departure and deep
goodbyes, pleased to have spent
these bowered hours
here, where Time goes un-
surmised and the seasons sleep.

Kindling

"She's just a girl," we cheerfully
chanted whenever one
of that ilk fumbled a grounder
or let a pop-fly drop
like a wounded duck, but there came
a day when they were more
than merely pert or plucky,
when curves emerged in the
most pleasing of places
and bangs became curls,
igniting a face, and something
akin to lust (or its whiff)
in the silken glances they gifted us -
kindled, and sang.

Ruby

Ruby Carr was our resident
ragpicker, gathering
cast-offs and hand-me-
downs wherever she could find them,
and she travelled from door to door
and pillar to post on her battered
bike, pinned together
by rivets of rust, with a jaunty
bell she'd ring at passers-by
just to hear it jingle,
and we often wondered what
became of all that fugitive
flotsam: a quilt big enough
to cover quintuplets or a Joseph's
coat for her only begotten
or the tangled tail of a kite
riding the bite of the wind?
And there was such exuberance
in the grin she gave us daily:
one that said simply,
"Be what you are."

A Valentine

For Anne in loving memory

You didn't approve of valentines
and the saccharine of their sentiments,
but I bought you a dozen roses
anyway, just to say
I approve of you, and love.

Bottle

For Bonnie and Sharon Laur

They were not related to the
chocolate-box lady,
but the sisters Laur played
bouncy-ball against
the wall next door
as if they were, pirouetting
prettily just in time
to cuddle a catch, contrive
a lithe leg-over or risk a
behind-the-back snatch,
and singing lustily the while,
like girls with moxy and bottle
galore and all contenders
aboard: "One, two, three
a-Laura See-cord!"

Girls' Game

Molly Gilbert is squatting
on her front walk, only
the blue-eyed dart
of her eyes, alive, and the flick
of her better hand, as quick
as a toad's tongue surprising
a fly – to catch some
six-pronged object
before the next bounce
of her one-ounce ball,
and, of course, I can see
no sense in such puerile
plucking or the joy of jostling
a jack, but then, I'm just
a boy, and it's a girls'
game.

Serene

We slept in narrow beds
no more than a yard of dark
between us, and I heard
your lallling and the side to side
in tune with the rhythmic rocking
of your head upon a pillow,
as if you might keep the Bogeyman
at bay, while I, to no avail,
toss and turn in search of
some narcotic drop
to put me under for the night,
but soon the rocking stopped,
and in the silken soft
of the silence, I heard you sigh
serenely into sleep.

Hope
With a nod to John Keats

This tufted titmouse,
teetering on a cherry-tree
bough just beyond
the reach of my window, sings
of summer and the season's ease
with a cherubic, two-fluted
note, but he is no nightingale
to tease a Keats awake
to the world and the melodious
verve of its verse, and yet
there is something in that solitary,
celibate song, a-thrum
in his throat, that touches on
Time and Eternity, and reminds us
of Beauty's bright brevity
and the welcome its wound,
and gives us reason to hope,
and be.

Camouflage

Oh, how we pored over the
petticoat pages of Grandma's
catalogue, prepared to faint
dead away, should a
nipple go naughtily budding
under the camouflaging
ripple of silk, or a knee
nudge just above
the photo's brimmed bottom,
and what we couldn't see
or judge to be deemed worthy
of prurient pursuit, we let
our dreams define, happy
to have them seethe inside
like a saint's tortured mortification,
or rub raw the nascent
nub of our 'unlawful'
lusts.

Paradisians

When Adam awoke in Eden
and noticed he wasn't alone,
did he greet his co-paradisian
with, "Madam, I'm Adam," and did Eve
reply, "Pardon the nudity,
but we're just as God wrought us,"
and did she blush when the riposte
came thus: "I wouldn't wish it
otherwise, for you are delicious
and I'm no prude."

Rooted

I have such a need to compose
a poem that will sing to the centuries,
one that is rooted true
in the hallowed ground of hearth
and home, and I would travail
the Seven Seas, trawling
for truths to feed its fury,
until my blood aborts
or my bones bleed, and when
my muse no longer endues
and after all is said
and done, I'll put down
my pen, pose for the loges,
and see how it goes.

Wordsworthian

I can still recall the first
scribble of mine to preen
in print: a homage to the
fallen of our two wars,
placed primly on the front
page of the local rag
to mark Remembrance Day,
and, just sixteen, I thought
I might be a budding bard,
with fame looming, but it was
three years hence
before I found again
the instinct for inking my world,
took up my nib and promulgated
an ode, worthy of Wordsworth
at his worst, and let it burst
into dubious bloom.

Tailor-Made

Mom smoked Buckinghams
because her lungs glowed
with each decent puff,
while Dad preferred Players
Navy Cut with the bearded
tar staring him down,
Uncle Bill brandished
the Lucky Strikes he'd smuggled
in across the River,
Gramps rolled his own
every Saturday evening
at the kitchen table, licking
the cigarette paper with the tip
of his talented tongue, and sprinkling
just enough of Ogden's
finest to make a satisfying
fag, after which,
he'd smile my way and declare:
"There it is, Donny,
better than tailor-made."

Slant
With a nod to Emily Dickinson

I've laboured a lifetime
trawling for the slanted candor
only poems supply
with potent trope and ruthless
rhyme, and I hope they will all
unwomb their truths
and bloom before I die.

An Innocent Eye

I don't quite recall
the moment when I first laid
an innocent eye upon
the great Lake that circled
my world like a seventh sea,
or strolled boldly barefoot
through its foaming breakers
and let them tousle on my toes,
or when I found courage
enough to wade into that
billowing chill, batten
on its buoyancy or press
a shoulder against the hoarded
warmth of an antediluvian
dune – but even then,
as now, I will never
allow my Lake to become
just another everyday
humdrum wonder
as I feel my soul leavening
in the sunlight, shimmering
in the dim of the blue-below.

Shockwaves

Being un-sistered as I was,
girls were to me foreign
territory, as exotic as pink
flamingoes posing on a pond
or spotted swans adrift
beside them: the doors
to our school were gendered in cement
and the yards, male and female
fiefdoms, *our* hair was brushed
tufted, *theirs,* freely
afloat, *they* wore fancy
frocks, *we* settled for humdrum
shirts and tepid trousers,
and though we played the others'
games, bouncy-ball
for us and aggies off-the-wall
for them, each platoon
rowed its own boat -
until the day an upturned
nose or wayward wink
sent shockwaves through the
system, like a blistered bliss,
and nothing was ever the same.

Drowned Aloud

Whenever Gran baked
a batch of peanut-butter
treats, the word went out
from street to street, and half-
a-dozen hopefuls, like new-
hatched friends or spaniels
on the spoor (tongues aflutter)
found their way to Gran's
verandah, where, cookies
in hand, I danced like His Nibs
on a dais – drowned aloud
in "Dibs!"

Chintzed

For my grandmother in loving memory

Gran's front room,
chintzed and royally rugged,
was reserved for special guests,
like the insurance-man with his thick-
fanned coupons-book
or the widow McCleister seeking
solace, or the Reverend Stone,
Anglican down to his ankles,
and though she wasn't convinced
that Jesus deserved all the
to-dos and ballyhoo heaped
upon Him, and that the Lord
was nothing to write-home-
about, she nevertheless
put the kettle on for the
importuning parson, and hedged
her bets.

When Lilacs Hung Lovely

When lilacs hung lovely
on their hedges and honeybees
busy-bodied among
pistil-fisted bloom
and petalled pollen, hectic
on nectar, and dandelions
dotted the lawn like spun
suns, and the Manitoba
maples unleashed their leaves
in green-thumbed penumbras,
I plundered this paradisal
plot like a bliss-jarred
bard, a-brim with limns
and similes heathen enough
to ruffle in the womb of the world.

Dervish

For my father in loving memory

You could strum a ukulele
like someone from the Islands,
sing like Bing (and out-
hum him), shoot pool
for pocket-money before
you could vote, and even then,
ice was your element (I can
feel the bite of your blades
and their urgent, sturdy
striding), and you were the
hometown hero,
praised everywhere in print
and furred photos, the village
rink incubating fame
and raucous applause , and who
among your antic fans
cared that you failed Grade
Eight three times
when you could skate like a
Dervish on a dare and dipsy-
doodle like the Rocket with his brooding
brows, and O what disappointment
when you chose the Air Force
and war above the pros
and a cozy career, leaving me
(not yet three) to wonder
where you went and who
you might be.

Something in my Throat

And when I was finally eight,
I found myself climbing
the back stairs from Gran's
kitchen to ours in time
to spot my mother's face
above me, some secret
excitement brimming in her eyes,
"Come on up," she was saying,
"I want you to meet your Dad,"
and when I peered over the
banister, I noticed a man,
tanned and blue-tunicked,
smiling as if he owned me,
"And you can call him that,"
she added, but the word choked
on something in my throat.

Love's Tug

I grew up calling my grandfather
"Pop" because I saw him
as the perfect version of myself
I wished to grow into –
a man good with his hands
over the lathe in his Saturday-
morning workshop
or curling around me
to steady the tot on his knee
while he recited the story
of the "Three Bears", doing
the voices of Mama and Papa
and the peevish squeak of Baby
Bruin at the sight of his purloined
porridge and shredded bed,
raising his eyebrows
like Goldilocks's glee at seeing
such potluck provisions and free
to behave badly, or the shaggy-
dog saga of the "Three
Little Pigs" and the brilliance
of brick over sticks and flawed
wolf-strewn straw, and O
how I giggled at the huffing and puffing
he manufactured for me,
and the tickle of his fingers along
my thigh as the piglets skittered
from stye to stye, and though
he wasn't one to hug,
I felt the tug of his love
just the same.

Brooder

For my father in loving memory

My Dad let me watch
as he built us a brooder hutch
in the backyard, where his new-
hatched Barred Rocks,
now fully fletched,
could roost in summery comfort—
fitting slim lozenges
lovingly into place with cut-
and-dried precision, and leaving
just enough apace
between slats for the breeze
to breathe and the sun incubate,
but while he tinkered and eyed
his artistry like a moody
Michelangelo, the chicks
died.

Odes
With a nod to John Keats

The poets of old let
their odes unfold slowly
into bloom, like Pindar's
strophe and antistrophe
in tripled antiphony
or the wrought apostrophes
of Horace to Rome and its
felicities before the Sabine
beckoned, or William's timid
intimations of that unknowable
abode beyond our being,
but you, Keats, beatified
birdsong and marbled urns
in melodious rhyme –
too sweet to be unheard.

When I am Gone

When I am gone and the bones
which kept my body upright
and ept are feeding the flames
that will render me ash to furnish
an urn, the million million
thoughts I've distilled in the mnemonics
of my mind will float free
and fend for themselves
unless, as I often suppose,
they've found some solace in the
havened home of my poems.

What Is

When lilacs lit up the hedges
that hugged my only home,
the air above them bloomed
with bees and their dozen, buzzing
cousins, and the leaves of the twinned
maples that arched, intimate,
over them shook like the sneeze
of a Pentecost wind, and I probed
this paradisal room
like an unsprung bard,
trawling the world for words
to say what is, and was.

Hunter's Heart

For my father in loving memory

Dad and I on the prowl
for rabbit or anything else
in the countryside a twelve-
gauge might gut, kicking
brush-piles, briared or not,
and waiting for that first
elastic leap and zigzagging
dart, and when my Dad
shouts "Shoot!" the critter
is a blur in my sights, and all
my thought of chocolate
bunnies in Easter baskets
or cuddly cottontails
curled in their burrows
flutter and freeze, and I am
as shocked to hear the shot
shudder my shoulder as the fleeing
felon (still lapping himself)
and a father with a hunter's hap-
hazard heart.

Somewhere

For Loretta Lynn in memoriam

You put the lilt in lyric
and the grunt in Country – a daughter
of Kentucky cornfields
and coal mines that blackened
lungs before their time,
and humped 'hollers', brushed
by their own breeze, and out of
these rich beginnings
something like song found
hope in your throat, and you
let it thrash there
like an untethered tongue,
and transfused its bold belling
into melodies a Muse might envy,
and I see you still, spot-lit
on a stage somewhere a stone's
throw from Heaven, and hear
all the songs you've left
unsung.

On The Road Again

For Anne in loving memory

We were just companions,
and me just someone
to ride shotgun
on our way to Hog Town
in the velvet breeze of your brand-
new Beetle, and once
there, we sat side
by cordial side through the
strangled angst of "Long
Day's Journey into Night;"
or sauntered the ROM, where T-
Rex bared the tantrum
of his teeth and grinned
his frozen bones; or gazed
AGO at the brooding loom
of "Crows Over a Cornfield"
or "Sunflowers" stunned
golden by the lash of light;
or aloft in the concert "gods,"
(your hand softening sudden
in mine) and we are awash
in the soaring chords of Ludwig's
"Ninth;" or dazzled by the
dithyrambic dance
of Maya Plistiskaya or weeping
at Mimi's dying diminuendo;
and some time thereafter,
to nobody's surprise,
love begat, and brimmed.

Box Cars

For Anne in loving memory

I was just a kid from the
countryside while you were
toasting your toes in Tinsel
Town, but soon we were romping
in the Rom, sassy in Massey,
Van-Goghing the AGO
or ambling Avenue Road
in taut besotted tandem,
and though we both believed
that girls belonged to Venus
and boys to Mars, we gambled
on Love and came up
Box Cars!

Well-Dug

For my father in loving memory

My Dad judged that if
he dug us a well, he'd
hit water at nineteen feet,
but didn't account for the
thousand ounces of blue
sludge that clung to spade
and tine like glutinous glue,
and a yard down and a yard
wide, he called it quits,
and when the rains came,
as they are wont to do,
and filled that pitted pocket
to the brim, deep enough
to drown a Daimler, it sat there
sulking in the sun, day
after day - mocking him.

Tethered

For my Uncle Potsy in loving memory

And here we are again
on the Lambton links, meandering
its manicured meadows on the trail
of a dimpled orb no bigger
than a numbed thumb – happy
just to be here and together
on such an amiable amble,
and when we pause to play,
as we must, I watch, in evident
awe, the wedge in your feathered
grip and the way you let it
find an arc with thrust
enough to stroke the ball
and send it like a lark on weathering
wings into the upper echelons
of air, where it hovers above
the distant green before dropping
daintily an inch from the pin,
and the grin we exchange is more
about love than the game, for we
have travelled the home-roads,
as tethered as twins.

Don Gutteridge was born in Sarnia and raised in the nearby village of Point Edward. He taught High School English for seven years, later becoming a Professor in the Faculty of Education at Western University, where he is now Professor Emeritus. He is the author of more than seventy books: poetry, fiction and scholarly works in pedagogical theory and practice. He has published eighty books; twenty-two novels, including the twelve-volume Marc Edwards mystery series, and forty seven books of poetry, one of which, Coppermine, was short-listed for the 1973 Governor-General's Award. In 1970 he won the UWO President's Medal for the best periodical poem of that year, "Death at Quebec."

Don lives in London, Ontario.

519-873-1585
gutteridgedonald@gmail.com